Home Maintenance
LOG BOOK

This Log Book Belongs to

....

Home Maintenance Log

MAINTENANCE FOR

DETAILS

DATE _____
PHONE _____
SKETCH DETAIL _____
SYSTEM APPLIANCE _____

PROBLEM _____
_____
_____
_____

PREPARATION

HOW WAS IT RESOLVED?

Home Maintenance Log

MAINTENANCE FOR

DETAILS

DATE _____
PHONE _____
SKETCH DETAIL _____
SYSTEM APPLIANCE _____

PROBLEM _____
_____
_____
_____

PREPARATION

HOW WAS IT RESOLVED?

Home Maintenance Log

MAINTENANCE FOR

DETAILS

DATE _____

PHONE _____

SKETCH DETAIL _____

SYSTEM APPLIANCE _____
_____

PROBLEM _____
_____
_____
_____

PREPARATION

HOW WAS IT RESOLVED?

Home Maintenance Log

MAINTENANCE FOR

DETAILS

DATE _____

PHONE _____

SKETCH DETAIL _____

SYSTEM APPLIANCE _____

PROBLEM _____

PREPARATION

HOW WAS IT RESOLVED?

Home Maintenance Log

MAINTENANCE FOR

DETAILS

DATE _____
PHONE _____
SKETCH DETAIL _____
SYSTEM APPLIANCE _____
_____
PROBLEM _____
_____
_____
_____

PREPARATION

HOW WAS IT RESOLVED?

Home Maintenance Log

MAINTENANCE FOR

DETAILS

DATE _____

PHONE _____

SKETCH DETAIL _____

SYSTEM APPLIANCE _____

_____

PROBLEM _____

_____

_____

_____

PREPARATION

HOW WAS IT RESOLVED?

Home Maintenance Log

MAINTENANCE FOR

DETAILS

DATE _____

PHONE _____

SKETCH DETAIL _____

SYSTEM APPLIANCE _____
_____

PROBLEM _____
_____
_____
_____

PREPARATION

HOW WAS IT RESOLVED?

Home Maintenance Log

MAINTENANCE FOR

DETAILS

DATE _____
PHONE _____
SKETCH DETAIL _____
SYSTEM APPLIANCE _____

PROBLEM _____
_____
_____
_____
_____

PREPARATION

HOW WAS IT RESOLVED?

Home Maintenance Log

MAINTENANCE FOR

DETAILS

DATE _____

PHONE _____

SKETCH DETAIL _____

SYSTEM APPLIANCE _____

_____

PROBLEM _____

_____

_____

_____

PREPARATION

HOW WAS IT RESOLVED?

Home Maintenance Log

MAINTENANCE FOR

DETAILS

DATE _____

PHONE _____

SKETCH DETAIL _____

SYSTEM APPLIANCE _____
_____

PROBLEM _____
_____
_____
_____

PREPARATION

HOW WAS IT RESOLVED?

Home Maintenance Log

MAINTENANCE FOR

DETAILS

DATE _____
PHONE _____
SKETCH DETAIL _____
SYSTEM APPLIANCE _____
_____
PROBLEM _____
_____
_____
_____

PREPARATION

HOW WAS IT RESOLVED?

Home Maintenance Log

MAINTENANCE FOR

DETAILS

DATE _____
PHONE _____
SKETCH DETAIL _____
SYSTEM APPLIANCE _____
_____
PROBLEM _____
_____
_____
_____

PREPARATION

HOW WAS IT RESOLVED?

Home Maintenance Log

MAINTENANCE FOR

DETAILS

DATE _____
PHONE _____
SKETCH DETAIL _____
SYSTEM APPLIANCE _____
_____

PROBLEM _____
_____
_____
_____

PREPARATION

HOW WAS IT RESOLVED?

Home Maintenance Log

MAINTENANCE FOR

DETAILS

DATE _____
PHONE _____
SKETCH DETAIL _____
SYSTEM APPLIANCE _____
_____
PROBLEM _____
_____
_____
_____

PREPARATION

HOW WAS IT RESOLVED?

Home Maintenance Log

MAINTENANCE FOR

DETAILS

DATE _____
PHONE _____
SKETCH DETAIL _____
SYSTEM APPLIANCE _____

PROBLEM _____
_____
_____
_____

PREPARATION

HOW WAS IT RESOLVED?

Home Maintenance Log

MAINTENANCE FOR

DETAILS

DATE _____
PHONE _____
SKETCH DETAIL _____
SYSTEM APPLIANCE _____

PROBLEM _____
_____
_____
_____

PREPARATION

HOW WAS IT RESOLVED?

Home Maintenance Log

MAINTENANCE FOR

DETAILS

DATE _____

PHONE _____

SKETCH DETAIL _____

SYSTEM APPLIANCE _____
_____

PROBLEM _____
_____
_____
_____

PREPARATION

HOW WAS IT RESOLVED?

Home Maintenance Log

MAINTENANCE FOR

DETAILS

DATE _____
PHONE _____
SKETCH DETAIL _____
SYSTEM APPLIANCE _____

PROBLEM _____
_____
_____
_____

PREPARATION

HOW WAS IT RESOLVED?

Home Maintenance Log

MAINTENANCE FOR

DETAILS

DATE _____

PHONE _____

SKETCH DETAIL _____

SYSTEM APPLIANCE _____
_____

PROBLEM _____
_____
_____
_____

PREPARATION

HOW WAS IT RESOLVED?

Home Maintenance Log

MAINTENANCE FOR

DETAILS

DATE _____
PHONE _____
SKETCH DETAIL _____
SYSTEM APPLIANCE _____

PROBLEM _____
_____
_____
_____

PREPARATION

HOW WAS IT RESOLVED?

 Home Maintenance Log

MAINTENANCE FOR

DETAILS

DATE _____
PHONE _____
SKETCH DETAIL _____
SYSTEM APPLIANCE _____
_____
PROBLEM _____
_____
_____
_____

PREPARATION

HOW WAS IT RESOLVED?

Home Maintenance Log

MAINTENANCE FOR

DETAILS

DATE _____
PHONE _____
SKETCH DETAIL _____
SYSTEM APPLIANCE _____
_____
PROBLEM _____
_____
_____
_____

PREPARATION

HOW WAS IT RESOLVED?

Home Maintenance Log

MAINTENANCE FOR

DETAILS

DATE _____
PHONE _____
SKETCH DETAIL _____
SYSTEM APPLIANCE _____
_____
PROBLEM _____
_____
_____
_____

PREPARATION

HOW WAS IT RESOLVED?

Home Maintenance Log

MAINTENANCE FOR

DETAILS

DATE _____
PHONE _____
SKETCH DETAIL _____
SYSTEM APPLIANCE _____
_____
PROBLEM _____
_____
_____
_____

PREPARATION

HOW WAS IT RESOLVED?

Home Maintenance Log

MAINTENANCE FOR

DETAILS

DATE _____

PHONE _____

SKETCH DETAIL _____

SYSTEM APPLIANCE _____

PROBLEM _____

PREPARATION

HOW WAS IT RESOLVED?

Home Maintenance Log

MAINTENANCE FOR

DETAILS

DATE _____
PHONE _____
SKETCH DETAIL _____
SYSTEM APPLIANCE _____
_____
PROBLEM _____
_____
_____
_____

PREPARATION

HOW WAS IT RESOLVED?

Home Maintenance Log

MAINTENANCE FOR

DETAILS

DATE _____
PHONE _____
SKETCH DETAIL _____
SYSTEM APPLIANCE _____
_____
PROBLEM _____
_____
_____
_____

PREPARATION

HOW WAS IT RESOLVED?

Home Maintenance Log

MAINTENANCE FOR

DETAILS

DATE _____
PHONE _____
SKETCH DETAIL _____
SYSTEM APPLIANCE _____

PROBLEM _____
_____
_____
_____

PREPARATION

HOW WAS IT RESOLVED?

Home Maintenance Log

MAINTENANCE FOR

DETAILS

DATE _____
PHONE _____
SKETCH DETAIL _____
SYSTEM APPLIANCE _____
_____
PROBLEM _____
_____
_____
_____

PREPARATION

HOW WAS IT RESOLVED?

Home Maintenance Log

MAINTENANCE FOR

DETAILS

DATE _____
PHONE _____
SKETCH DETAIL _____
SYSTEM APPLIANCE _____
_____
PROBLEM _____
_____
_____
_____

PREPARATION

HOW WAS IT RESOLVED?

Home Maintenance Log

MAINTENANCE FOR

DETAILS

DATE _____

PHONE _____

SKETCH DETAIL _____

SYSTEM APPLIANCE _____

PROBLEM _____

PREPARATION

HOW WAS IT RESOLVED?

Home Maintenance Log

MAINTENANCE FOR

DETAILS

DATE _____
PHONE _____
SKETCH DETAIL _____
SYSTEM APPLIANCE _____
_____
PROBLEM _____
_____
_____
_____

PREPARATION

HOW WAS IT RESOLVED?

Home Maintenance Log

MAINTENANCE FOR

DETAILS

DATE _____
PHONE _____
SKETCH DETAIL _____
SYSTEM APPLIANCE _____
_____
PROBLEM _____
_____
_____
_____

PREPARATION

HOW WAS IT RESOLVED?

Home Maintenance Log

MAINTENANCE FOR

DETAILS

DATE _____
PHONE _____
SKETCH DETAIL _____
SYSTEM APPLIANCE _____
_____
PROBLEM _____
_____
_____
_____

PREPARATION

HOW WAS IT RESOLVED?

Home Maintenance Log

MAINTENANCE FOR

DETAILS

DATE _____
PHONE _____
SKETCH DETAIL _____
SYSTEM APPLIANCE _____

PROBLEM _____
_____
_____
_____

PREPARATION

HOW WAS IT RESOLVED?

# Home Maintenance Log

MAINTENANCE FOR

DETAILS

DATE _____
PHONE _____
SKETCH DETAIL _____
SYSTEM APPLIANCE _____

PROBLEM _____
_____
_____
_____

PREPARATION

HOW WAS IT RESOLVED?

 Home Maintenance Log

MAINTENANCE FOR

DETAILS

DATE _____
PHONE _____
SKETCH DETAIL _____
SYSTEM APPLIANCE _____
_____
PROBLEM _____
_____
_____
_____

PREPARATION

HOW WAS IT RESOLVED?

Home Maintenance Log

MAINTENANCE FOR

DETAILS

DATE _____
PHONE _____
SKETCH DETAIL _____
SYSTEM APPLIANCE _____
_____
PROBLEM _____
_____
_____
_____

PREPARATION

HOW WAS IT RESOLVED?

Home Maintenance Log

MAINTENANCE FOR

DETAILS

DATE _____

PHONE _____

SKETCH DETAIL _____

SYSTEM APPLIANCE _____
_____

PROBLEM _____
_____
_____
_____

PREPARATION

HOW WAS IT RESOLVED?

Home Maintenance Log

MAINTENANCE FOR

DETAILS

DATE _____

PHONE _____

SKETCH DETAIL _____

SYSTEM APPLIANCE _____

PROBLEM _____
_____
_____
_____

PREPARATION

HOW WAS IT RESOLVED?

 Home Maintenance Log

MAINTENANCE FOR

DETAILS

DATE _____
PHONE _____
SKETCH DETAIL _____
SYSTEM APPLIANCE _____
_____
PROBLEM _____
_____
_____
_____

PREPARATION

HOW WAS IT RESOLVED?

Home Maintenance Log

MAINTENANCE FOR

DETAILS

DATE _____
PHONE _____
SKETCH DETAIL _____
SYSTEM APPLIANCE _____

PROBLEM _____
_____
_____
_____

PREPARATION

HOW WAS IT RESOLVED?

Home Maintenance Log

MAINTENANCE FOR

DETAILS

DATE _____

PHONE _____

SKETCH DETAIL _____

SYSTEM APPLIANCE _____

PROBLEM _____
_____
_____
_____

PREPARATION

HOW WAS IT RESOLVED?

Home Maintenance Log

MAINTENANCE FOR

DETAILS

DATE _____
PHONE _____
SKETCH DETAIL _____
SYSTEM APPLIANCE _____
_____

PROBLEM _____
_____
_____
_____

PREPARATION

HOW WAS IT RESOLVED?

Home Maintenance Log

MAINTENANCE FOR

DETAILS

DATE _____

PHONE _____

SKETCH DETAIL _____

SYSTEM APPLIANCE _____
_____

PROBLEM _____
_____
_____
_____

PREPARATION

HOW WAS IT RESOLVED?

Home Maintenance Log

MAINTENANCE FOR

DETAILS

DATE _____
PHONE _____
SKETCH DETAIL _____
SYSTEM APPLIANCE _____
_____
PROBLEM _____
_____
_____
_____

PREPARATION

HOW WAS IT RESOLVED?

Home Maintenance Log

MAINTENANCE FOR

DETAILS

DATE _____

PHONE _____

SKETCH DETAIL _____

SYSTEM APPLIANCE _____

PROBLEM _____

PREPARATION

HOW WAS IT RESOLVED?

Home Maintenance Log

MAINTENANCE FOR

DETAILS

DATE _____
PHONE _____
SKETCH DETAIL _____
SYSTEM APPLIANCE _____
_____
PROBLEM _____
_____
_____
_____

PREPARATION

HOW WAS IT RESOLVED?

Home Maintenance Log

MAINTENANCE FOR

DETAILS

DATE _____
PHONE _____
SKETCH DETAIL _____
SYSTEM APPLIANCE _____
_____
PROBLEM _____
_____
_____
_____

PREPARATION

HOW WAS IT RESOLVED?

Home Maintenance Log

MAINTENANCE FOR

DETAILS

DATE _____
PHONE _____
SKETCH DETAIL _____
SYSTEM APPLIANCE _____
_____

PROBLEM _____
_____
_____
_____

PREPARATION

HOW WAS IT RESOLVED?

Home Maintenance Log

MAINTENANCE FOR

DETAILS

DATE _____

PHONE _____

SKETCH DETAIL _____

SYSTEM APPLIANCE _____

_____

PROBLEM _____

_____

_____

_____

PREPARATION

HOW WAS IT RESOLVED?

Home Maintenance Log

MAINTENANCE FOR

DETAILS

DATE _____
PHONE _____
SKETCH DETAIL _____
SYSTEM APPLIANCE _____
_____
PROBLEM _____
_____
_____
_____

PREPARATION

HOW WAS IT RESOLVED?

Home Maintenance Log

MAINTENANCE FOR

DETAILS

DATE _____

PHONE _____

SKETCH DETAIL _____

SYSTEM APPLIANCE _____

_____

PROBLEM _____

_____

_____

_____

PREPARATION

HOW WAS IT RESOLVED?

Home Maintenance Log

MAINTENANCE FOR

DETAILS

DATE _____
PHONE _____
SKETCH DETAIL _____
SYSTEM APPLIANCE _____
_____
PROBLEM _____
_____
_____
_____

PREPARATION

HOW WAS IT RESOLVED?

Home Maintenance Log

MAINTENANCE FOR

DETAILS

DATE _____
PHONE _____
SKETCH DETAIL _____
SYSTEM APPLIANCE _____
_____
PROBLEM _____
_____
_____
_____

PREPARATION

HOW WAS IT RESOLVED?

# Home Maintenance Log

MAINTENANCE FOR

DETAILS

DATE _____
PHONE _____
SKETCH DETAIL _____
SYSTEM APPLIANCE _____
_____
PROBLEM _____
_____
_____
_____

PREPARATION

HOW WAS IT RESOLVED?

Home Maintenance Log

MAINTENANCE FOR

DETAILS

DATE _____
PHONE _____
SKETCH DETAIL _____
SYSTEM APPLIANCE _____
_____
PROBLEM _____
_____
_____
_____

PREPARATION

HOW WAS IT RESOLVED?

Home Maintenance Log

MAINTENANCE FOR

DETAILS

DATE _____
PHONE _____
SKETCH DETAIL _____
SYSTEM APPLIANCE _____
_____
PROBLEM _____
_____
_____
_____

PREPARATION

HOW WAS IT RESOLVED?

Home Maintenance Log

MAINTENANCE FOR

DETAILS

DATE _____

PHONE _____

SKETCH DETAIL _____

SYSTEM APPLIANCE _____

PROBLEM _____
_____
_____
_____

PREPARATION

HOW WAS IT RESOLVED?

Home Maintenance Log

MAINTENANCE FOR

DETAILS

DATE _____
PHONE _____
SKETCH DETAIL _____
SYSTEM APPLIANCE _____
_____
PROBLEM _____
_____
_____
_____

PREPARATION

HOW WAS IT RESOLVED?

Home Maintenance Log

MAINTENANCE FOR

DETAILS

DATE _____
PHONE _____
SKETCH DETAIL _____
SYSTEM APPLIANCE _____
_____
PROBLEM _____
_____
_____
_____

PREPARATION

HOW WAS IT RESOLVED?

MAINTENANCE FOR

DETAILS

DATE _____
PHONE _____
SKETCH DETAIL _____
SYSTEM APPLIANCE _____
_____
PROBLEM _____
_____
_____
_____

PREPARATION

HOW WAS IT RESOLVED?

Home Maintenance Log

MAINTENANCE FOR

DETAILS

DATE _____

PHONE _____

SKETCH DETAIL _____

SYSTEM APPLIANCE _____
_____

PROBLEM _____
_____
_____
_____

PREPARATION

HOW WAS IT RESOLVED?

Home Maintenance Log

MAINTENANCE FOR

DETAILS

DATE _____
PHONE _____
SKETCH DETAIL _____
SYSTEM APPLIANCE _____
_____
PROBLEM _____
_____
_____
_____

PREPARATION

HOW WAS IT RESOLVED?

Home Maintenance Log

MAINTENANCE FOR

DETAILS

DATE _____
PHONE _____
SKETCH DETAIL _____
SYSTEM APPLIANCE _____
_____
PROBLEM _____
_____
_____
_____

PREPARATION

HOW WAS IT RESOLVED?

Home Maintenance Log

MAINTENANCE FOR

DETAILS

DATE _____
PHONE _____
SKETCH DETAIL _____
SYSTEM APPLIANCE _____
_____
PROBLEM _____
_____
_____
_____

PREPARATION

HOW WAS IT RESOLVED?

Home Maintenance Log

MAINTENANCE FOR

DETAILS

DATE _____
PHONE _____
SKETCH DETAIL _____
SYSTEM APPLIANCE _____
_____
PROBLEM _____
_____
_____
_____

PREPARATION

HOW WAS IT RESOLVED?

Home Maintenance Log

MAINTENANCE FOR

DETAILS

DATE _____
PHONE _____
SKETCH DETAIL _____
SYSTEM APPLIANCE _____
_____
PROBLEM _____
_____
_____
_____

PREPARATION

HOW WAS IT RESOLVED?

Home Maintenance Log

MAINTENANCE FOR

DETAILS

DATE _____

PHONE _____

SKETCH DETAIL _____

SYSTEM APPLIANCE _____

PROBLEM _____
_____
_____
_____

PREPARATION

HOW WAS IT RESOLVED?

# Home Maintenance Log

MAINTENANCE FOR

DETAILS

DATE _____

PHONE _____

SKETCH DETAIL _____

SYSTEM APPLIANCE _____

PROBLEM _____

PREPARATION

HOW WAS IT RESOLVED?

Home Maintenance Log

MAINTENANCE FOR

DETAILS

DATE _____
PHONE _____
SKETCH DETAIL _____
SYSTEM APPLIANCE _____

PROBLEM _____

PREPARATION

HOW WAS IT RESOLVED?

Home Maintenance Log

MAINTENANCE FOR

DETAILS

DATE _____
PHONE _____
SKETCH DETAIL _____
SYSTEM APPLIANCE _____
_____
PROBLEM _____
_____
_____
_____

PREPARATION

HOW WAS IT RESOLVED?

Home Maintenance Log

MAINTENANCE FOR

DETAILS

DATE _____
PHONE _____
SKETCH DETAIL _____
SYSTEM APPLIANCE _____
_____
PROBLEM _____
_____
_____
_____

PREPARATION

HOW WAS IT RESOLVED?

Home Maintenance Log

MAINTENANCE FOR

DETAILS

DATE _____
PHONE _____
SKETCH DETAIL _____
SYSTEM APPLIANCE _____

PROBLEM _____
_____
_____
_____

PREPARATION

HOW WAS IT RESOLVED?

Home Maintenance Log

MAINTENANCE FOR

DETAILS

DATE _____
PHONE _____
SKETCH DETAIL _____
SYSTEM APPLIANCE _____
_____
PROBLEM _____
_____
_____
_____

PREPARATION

HOW WAS IT RESOLVED?

Home Maintenance Log

MAINTENANCE FOR

DETAILS

DATE _____
PHONE _____
SKETCH DETAIL _____
SYSTEM APPLIANCE _____
_____
PROBLEM _____
_____
_____
_____

PREPARATION

HOW WAS IT RESOLVED?

Home Maintenance Log

MAINTENANCE FOR

DETAILS

DATE _____
PHONE _____
SKETCH DETAIL _____
SYSTEM APPLIANCE _____
_____
PROBLEM _____
_____
_____
_____

PREPARATION

HOW WAS IT RESOLVED?

Home Maintenance Log

MAINTENANCE FOR

DETAILS

DATE _____
PHONE _____
SKETCH DETAIL _____
SYSTEM APPLIANCE _____
_____
PROBLEM _____
_____
_____
_____

PREPARATION

HOW WAS IT RESOLVED?

Home Maintenance Log

MAINTENANCE FOR

DETAILS

DATE _____
PHONE _____
SKETCH DETAIL _____
SYSTEM APPLIANCE _____
_____
PROBLEM _____
_____
_____
_____

PREPARATION

HOW WAS IT RESOLVED?

Home Maintenance Log

MAINTENANCE FOR

DETAILS

DATE _____
PHONE _____
SKETCH DETAIL _____
SYSTEM APPLIANCE _____

PROBLEM _____

PREPARATION

HOW WAS IT RESOLVED?

Home Maintenance Log

MAINTENANCE FOR

DETAILS

DATE _____

PHONE _____

SKETCH DETAIL _____

SYSTEM APPLIANCE _____

PROBLEM _____
_____
_____
_____

PREPARATION

HOW WAS IT RESOLVED?

Home Maintenance Log

MAINTENANCE FOR

DETAILS

DATE _____
PHONE _____
SKETCH DETAIL _____
SYSTEM APPLIANCE _____

PROBLEM _____
_____
_____
_____

PREPARATION

HOW WAS IT RESOLVED?

Home Maintenance Log

MAINTENANCE FOR

DETAILS

DATE _____
PHONE _____
SKETCH DETAIL _____
SYSTEM APPLIANCE _____

PROBLEM _____

PREPARATION

HOW WAS IT RESOLVED?

Home Maintenance Log

MAINTENANCE FOR

DETAILS

DATE _____
PHONE _____
SKETCH DETAIL _____
SYSTEM APPLIANCE _____
_____
PROBLEM _____
_____
_____
_____

PREPARATION

HOW WAS IT RESOLVED?

Home Maintenance Log

MAINTENANCE FOR

DETAILS

DATE _____
PHONE _____
SKETCH DETAIL _____
SYSTEM APPLIANCE _____
_____
PROBLEM _____
_____
_____
_____

PREPARATION

HOW WAS IT RESOLVED?

# Home Maintenance Log

MAINTENANCE FOR

DETAILS

DATE _____
PHONE _____
SKETCH DETAIL _____
SYSTEM APPLIANCE _____
_____
PROBLEM _____
_____
_____
_____

PREPARATION

HOW WAS IT RESOLVED?

Home Maintenance Log

MAINTENANCE FOR

DETAILS

DATE _____
PHONE _____
SKETCH DETAIL _____
SYSTEM APPLIANCE _____
_____
PROBLEM _____
_____
_____
_____

PREPARATION

HOW WAS IT RESOLVED?

Home Maintenance Log

MAINTENANCE FOR

DETAILS

DATE _____
PHONE _____
SKETCH DETAIL _____
SYSTEM APPLIANCE _____
_____
PROBLEM _____
_____
_____
_____

PREPARATION

HOW WAS IT RESOLVED?

 # Home Maintenance Log

MAINTENANCE FOR

DETAILS

DATE _____
PHONE _____
SKETCH DETAIL _____
SYSTEM APPLIANCE _____
_____
PROBLEM _____
_____
_____
_____

PREPARATION

HOW WAS IT RESOLVED?

Home Maintenance Log

MAINTENANCE FOR

DETAILS

DATE _____

PHONE _____

SKETCH DETAIL _____

SYSTEM APPLIANCE _____

_____

PROBLEM _____

_____

_____

_____

PREPARATION

HOW WAS IT RESOLVED?

Home Maintenance Log

MAINTENANCE FOR

DETAILS

DATE _____
PHONE _____
SKETCH DETAIL _____
SYSTEM APPLIANCE _____
_____
PROBLEM _____
_____
_____
_____

PREPARATION

HOW WAS IT RESOLVED?

Home Maintenance Log

MAINTENANCE FOR

DETAILS

DATE _____
PHONE _____
SKETCH DETAIL _____
SYSTEM APPLIANCE _____
_____
PROBLEM _____
_____
_____
_____

PREPARATION

HOW WAS IT RESOLVED?

Home Maintenance Log

MAINTENANCE FOR

DETAILS

DATE _____
PHONE _____
SKETCH DETAIL _____
SYSTEM APPLIANCE _____
_____
PROBLEM _____
_____
_____
_____

PREPARATION

HOW WAS IT RESOLVED?

Home Maintenance Log

MAINTENANCE FOR

DETAILS

DATE _____
PHONE _____
SKETCH DETAIL _____
SYSTEM APPLIANCE _____
_____
PROBLEM _____
_____
_____
_____

PREPARATION

HOW WAS IT RESOLVED?

Home Maintenance Log

MAINTENANCE FOR

DETAILS

DATE _____

PHONE _____

SKETCH DETAIL _____

SYSTEM APPLIANCE _____

_____

PROBLEM _____

_____

_____

_____

PREPARATION

HOW WAS IT RESOLVED?

Home Maintenance Log

MAINTENANCE FOR

DETAILS

DATE _____
PHONE _____
SKETCH DETAIL _____
SYSTEM APPLIANCE _____
_____
PROBLEM _____
_____
_____
_____

PREPARATION

HOW WAS IT RESOLVED?

MAINTENANCE FOR

DETAILS

DATE _____
PHONE _____
SKETCH DETAIL _____
SYSTEM APPLIANCE _____
_____
PROBLEM _____
_____
_____
_____

PREPARATION

HOW WAS IT RESOLVED?

Home Maintenance Log

MAINTENANCE FOR

DETAILS

DATE _____
PHONE _____
SKETCH DETAIL _____
SYSTEM APPLIANCE _____
_____
PROBLEM _____
_____
_____
_____

PREPARATION

HOW WAS IT RESOLVED?

Home Maintenance Log

MAINTENANCE FOR

DETAILS

DATE _____
PHONE _____
SKETCH DETAIL _____
SYSTEM APPLIANCE _____
_____
PROBLEM _____
_____
_____
_____

PREPARATION

HOW WAS IT RESOLVED?

Home Maintenance Log

MAINTENANCE FOR

DETAILS

DATE _____
PHONE _____
SKETCH DETAIL _____
SYSTEM APPLIANCE _____
_____
PROBLEM _____
_____
_____
_____

PREPARATION

HOW WAS IT RESOLVED?

Home Maintenance Log

MAINTENANCE FOR

DETAILS

DATE _____

PHONE _____

SKETCH DETAIL _____

SYSTEM APPLIANCE _____

PROBLEM _____
_____
_____
_____

PREPARATION

HOW WAS IT RESOLVED?

Home Maintenance Log

MAINTENANCE FOR

DETAILS

DATE _____

PHONE _____

SKETCH DETAIL _____

SYSTEM APPLIANCE _____

_____

PROBLEM _____

_____

_____

_____

PREPARATION

HOW WAS IT RESOLVED?

Home Maintenance Log

MAINTENANCE FOR

DETAILS

DATE _____

PHONE _____

SKETCH DETAIL _____

SYSTEM APPLIANCE _____
_____

PROBLEM _____
_____
_____
_____

PREPARATION

HOW WAS IT RESOLVED?

# Home Maintenance Log

MAINTENANCE FOR

DETAILS

DATE _____
PHONE _____
SKETCH DETAIL _____
SYSTEM APPLIANCE _____

PROBLEM _____
_____
_____
_____

PREPARATION

HOW WAS IT RESOLVED?

Home Maintenance Log

MAINTENANCE FOR

DETAILS

DATE _____
PHONE _____
SKETCH DETAIL _____
SYSTEM APPLIANCE _____
_____
PROBLEM _____
_____
_____
_____

PREPARATION

HOW WAS IT RESOLVED?

Home Maintenance Log

MAINTENANCE FOR

DETAILS

DATE _____
PHONE _____
SKETCH DETAIL _____
SYSTEM APPLIANCE _____
_____
PROBLEM _____
_____
_____
_____

PREPARATION

HOW WAS IT RESOLVED?

Home Maintenance Log

MAINTENANCE FOR

DETAILS

DATE _____

PHONE _____

SKETCH DETAIL _____

SYSTEM APPLIANCE _____

PROBLEM _____
_____
_____
_____

PREPARATION

HOW WAS IT RESOLVED?

Home Maintenance Log

MAINTENANCE FOR

DETAILS

DATE _____
PHONE _____
SKETCH DETAIL _____
SYSTEM APPLIANCE _____

PROBLEM _____
_____
_____
_____

PREPARATION

HOW WAS IT RESOLVED?

# Home Maintenance Log

MAINTENANCE FOR

DETAILS

DATE _____

PHONE _____

SKETCH DETAIL _____

SYSTEM APPLIANCE _____
_____

PROBLEM _____
_____
_____
_____

PREPARATION

HOW WAS IT RESOLVED?

Home Maintenance Log

MAINTENANCE FOR

DETAILS

DATE _____
PHONE _____
SKETCH DETAIL _____
SYSTEM APPLIANCE _____
_____
PROBLEM _____
_____
_____
_____

PREPARATION

HOW WAS IT RESOLVED?

Home Maintenance Log

MAINTENANCE FOR

DETAILS

DATE _____

PHONE _____

SKETCH DETAIL _____

SYSTEM APPLIANCE _____
_____

PROBLEM _____
_____
_____
_____

PREPARATION

HOW WAS IT RESOLVED?

Home Maintenance Log

MAINTENANCE FOR

DETAILS

DATE _____
PHONE _____
SKETCH DETAIL _____
SYSTEM APPLIANCE _____

PROBLEM _____
_____
_____
_____

PREPARATION

HOW WAS IT RESOLVED?

Home Maintenance Log

MAINTENANCE FOR

DETAILS

DATE _____
PHONE _____
SKETCH DETAIL _____
SYSTEM APPLIANCE _____
_____
PROBLEM _____
_____
_____
_____

PREPARATION

HOW WAS IT RESOLVED?

Home Maintenance Log

MAINTENANCE FOR

DETAILS

DATE _____
PHONE _____
SKETCH DETAIL _____
SYSTEM APPLIANCE _____
_____
PROBLEM _____
_____
_____
_____

PREPARATION

HOW WAS IT RESOLVED?

 # Home Maintenance Log

MAINTENANCE FOR

DETAILS

DATE _____

PHONE _____

SKETCH DETAIL _____

SYSTEM APPLIANCE _____
_____

PROBLEM _____
_____
_____
_____

PREPARATION

HOW WAS IT RESOLVED?

Home Maintenance Log

MAINTENANCE FOR

DETAILS

DATE _____

PHONE _____

SKETCH DETAIL _____

SYSTEM APPLIANCE _____

PROBLEM _____

PREPARATION

HOW WAS IT RESOLVED?

Home Maintenance Log

MAINTENANCE FOR

DETAILS

DATE _____
PHONE _____
SKETCH DETAIL _____
SYSTEM APPLIANCE _____
_____
PROBLEM _____
_____
_____
_____

PREPARATION

HOW WAS IT RESOLVED?

Home Maintenance Log

MAINTENANCE FOR

DETAILS

DATE _____
PHONE _____
SKETCH DETAIL _____
SYSTEM APPLIANCE _____
_____
PROBLEM _____
_____
_____
_____

PREPARATION

HOW WAS IT RESOLVED?

Home Maintenance Log

MAINTENANCE FOR

DETAILS

DATE _____
PHONE _____
SKETCH DETAIL _____
SYSTEM APPLIANCE _____
_____
PROBLEM _____
_____
_____
_____

PREPARATION

HOW WAS IT RESOLVED?

www.ingramcontent.com/pod-product-compliance
Lightning Source LLC
Chambersburg PA
CBHW050257120526
44590CB00016B/2384